Lips Open and Divine

Matthew A. Hamilton

Winter Goose
PUBLISHING
where words take flight

Winter Goose Publishing
45 Lafayette Road #114
North Hampton, NH 03862

www.wintergoosepublishing.com
Contact Information: info@wintergoosepublishing.com

Lips Open and Divine

First Edition, March 2016

Cover Design by Winter Goose Publishing
Typesetting by Odyssey Books

ISBN: 978-1-941058-42-8

Published in the United States of America

To Romekka, I love you

Contents

I

Snakes Belong in the Wild

As a child,
she kept purple-tailed lizards
in a doll house. The girls at school
called her Queen of the Reptiles.
A boy pulled a frog from his pocket
and told her to kiss it. She spit
in his face and disappeared
up a tree a maggot, wrapped herself
in bark-colored leaves
and waited for the bell to ring.
Years later, after college,
she disappeared again,
this time into the desert.
Her trailer was a rain forest.
She collected rattlers and corals,
mambas, and a Gaboon viper
she allowed to curl around her wrist
like a diamond bracelet.
She never invited guests,
the boys and girls from school
an unbroken reminder of provocation.
She was never reported missing
and her ears and nose thrashed red
for days like exotic butterflies in flight.

Benazir Bhutto

Muslim women don't drive cars.

She braced herself and got behind the wheel,
drove across the border into Pakistan, the sun
falling like a red marble behind the mountains.

She parked in Musharraf's driveway.

Living in exile for seven years
rewards patience, she said.

She shook his hand, feeling
the strength of the people.

He offered her tea.

She slapped his hand away.

The world behind the black veil is unclear.

Even if you ate grass for a thousand years
democracy would never grow here, he said.

Bullets are more popular than votes.

The people demand liberation, she said.
They cannot wait for change any longer.

The people should decide my fate, he said.
If death is what they want, stick a bomb
in my mouth and let my life end in tyranny.

Musharraf sipped his tea and smiled
like God facing a devoted enemy.

Transplant Tourism

Stepping off the train, you greeted me
with the four needy hands of the god Dhanvantari.

A kidney, you said,
and handed me money
to feed my family many months.

I'm honored you try to speak Hindi,
I said, *but I know English.*

Our words were two passing trains
inked on paper railroads.

I picked up my mat and followed you
to a room dug out from the side of a mountain.

On a steel table beside my bed,
knives shone like prayer temples.

I woke up and you were healing beside me,
your eyes blowfly eggs opening red.

My youngest removed the stitches
from your back as if mending a royal carpet,

blessing the stitches with fire
and blowing orange dust in the air,

then pressing her thumb into the mortar,
she painted your face with lotus breath
from Buddha's tomb,

and you were reborn,
ready to live a thousand years.

Operation Iraqi Freedom, 2003

I squeeze the trigger.

My arms ripple
like straw-colored streams.

The flag is now
the center of my memory,

and a teenage boy
with a poppy
blooming from his head.

Trafficked

She cut off her head
and filled it with water.

In whorls of three oleander leaves
shot from her fingers and toes.

A cluster of red flowers
bloomed from her hands.

She bled for her parents
because they were starving.

The man in a white cowboy hat
said red was his favorite color.

He teased her into a van
with a bundle of other girls.

When they crossed the border into Texas,
the van stopped and shivered with fear.

Vamanos, a man said,
and stuffed her in a sack.

When she woke up, she found
night crawling fingers building
a home between her legs.

She picked up a piece of glass
and jammed it in her wrist.

Her eyes bit down hard
as she thought of her father
sipping a cold Jarrito.

She listened to the silent wilderness.

Her blood smelled like moldy wood.

Mama's Funeral

When they opened the casket, I saw Mama's rosy cheeks. Her Spanish moss hair lay still on the pillow, helpless without the live oak and Alabama winds. She smelled like oatmeal. I said she was alive. Dad said she was dead. I touched her chest to make sure. Everyone watched me. I was only five. The old gossipy ladies from the ice-cream-social church committee smiled at me. Sad smiles. I slipped my hand into my pants pocket and hid the secrets of Mama's soul. She told me once heaven isn't far away, and if I ever wanted to visit her, just go out to the garden and listen to bee's wings drum against the apple blossoms. I returned to my seat and sat there quietly anticipating the crowd storming into my house, bayoneting the roast and smothering the mashed potatoes in blood-colored gravy. My hand never left my pocket.

Trilobite

for Steve Haworth

When I was seven,
my dad bought me a Skilsaw.

I carved out my name in the red wood
and played with its tissues.

My girlfriend held out her arm
and asked me to play with her.

Modified piercings are no joke, I said.
I might puncture a nerve, chop off a hand.

She rolled up her sleeve and said,
Pain makes me orgasm.

I made her a bracelet
and slipped it beneath her skin.
Her muscles, pink and gummy,
glowed like hot orange light

and, as I entered her,
ten billion suns exploded
like seminal atoms shooting across the stars.

Kentucky Briar, April 1975

Huddled nurses spooled in white
on a cracked sleet morning
holding Winston 100s
with uneasy hands,

mothers all of them,
their eyes bent to the east
mourning their sons
ten thousand miles away
in the syrupy rice fields
of Xuan Loc,

and me,
newly born,
nested in warm arms
and a jungle of blankets.

I arrived too late
to take a rifle
in my hands
and erase
what my mother
never had to imagine:

me in a rice field
cheek by jaw
with my brother,
our lives underneath
gurgling mud.

Witness

I remember the smell
from Dad's grease monkey uniform,
the black under his nails,
his eyes storybook devil red.

He accused Mom of sleeping
with the mailman,
and hit her with a tire iron.

Blood swam down the wall
like a school of redfish.

Then he came after me,
running so fast down the stairs
that he fell and twisted his ankle.

His pig eyes glazed over
and his nostrils vomited
the sour smell of whisky.

I walked up to him, slowly,
poked his shoulder,
thought about wrapping my arms
around his neck, forgiving him,
but my body was against it.

I stared at his hands,
the hands that taught me
to ride a bike, hugged me
after returning from Afghanistan.

They weren't the same hands.

I ran out the den door,
his voice as cold as thunder
trailing like IED shrapnel behind me.

Black Dolphin Prison

The star on my shoulder
says I will bow to no one.

Cop pulled me over
for a busted taillight.

I climbed out of the car
and sliced him open.

He was ruddy inside,
like cod. I was curious

and licked salty pieces
of him off my chubby fingers.

The cops found me
with his tongue in my hand.

Already turned cold, his skin
was as thin as a gnat's wing,
his eyes like shards of glass,
a blue-green shade
the color of his uniform.

The Lieutenant Guard
does not call me by name.

He says to speak it
makes his mouth bend backwards.

Bodhisattva, 1963

The road catches fire.

Black smoke

balloons over Thich Quang Duc

like a thousand hands praying.

Flames a tamed cat

crawling up quiet arms.

Lips never move.

A man photographed in ash.

Bangkok Bargirl

He sat at a table in Bangkok
across from a window
marketing anonymous girls
sucking their index fingers.
He chose the one
in the sunset-colored dress.
I speak no good English, she said.
You're so pretty you don't have to,
he said, and kissed her hand.
The manager pulled him away.
Touching costs more,
private room upstairs.
She rode him piggyback
to a bed dressed in silk
where they cocooned
their bodies in thanaka paste
and cucumber water.
I no like Thai man,
she nibbled in his ear.
He butterfly too much.
Me like farang, thank you mak mak.
He ignored her words,
jammed her nipple in his mouth.
In the morning,
she found a few extra baht
under her pillow.

You no like me,
take me to America?
Like you fine, he said,
and kissed her goodbye.
His departure slashed shame
across her enslaved cheekbone.
Her eyes proved that dreams
still exist. She sat in a circle
of candles, her naked body balanced
in prayer on the golden hair of Buddha.

Bad Voodoo

Jason wrapped a rosary
around his wrist
and blew fire in the air.

We both saw it at the same time:
a red Mercedes, hood up
on the side of the road,
smoking like an incense stick.

IED blew our Hummer sideways.
I jumped out and brushed the smoke off my arms.
Jason's eyes burned like votive candles. I plugged

his nose full of cotton like a Baron Semedi doll
and watched the spirits dance over his furious body.

II

Smoke Jumper

The orange earth below
burns of cities.

I see a buck
with flames on his back
jump into a river.

The wind blows his body
across the water
as if it's cottonwood seed.

His hooves spark the underbrush
and the fire is on me.

My eyes burn.
The universe ignites.

I curl into the water
like a pill bug,
thick with silver dust,
dig myself in,
and wait.

It starts to rain
by the time the chopper
touches down.

Aryan Brotherhood

Caught a nigger stealing drugs
from a shower room drain.

I wasn't looking for a fight.

Let me have them back
and you can go, I said.

He held up his fists
like a disobedient slave.

I felt my knuckleduster
vibrate off his forehead.

I leaned against his body
and waited for the dark sky to burn.

Somewhere there is a god
that agrees with what I have done.

Wiccan Suicide

The Wiccan hangs
from an apple tree.

Her eyes leak spiced cider.

Last breath
the color of a triple moon.

A family of grey hearts rest
on a cold table nearby.

There is no one left
in this world to love her.

The Middle-Way Approach

Every day I spin the prayer wheel.

I drink lotus water.

I shake hands with Xi Jinping.

I kneel before Buddha
in his fat asana.

I point my toes north
and march barefoot across the Great Wall.

The sun burns the wind.

Afghan National Army Soldier Admits Helping the Taliban

The Taliban buried my wife

in a poppy field neck deep,

and stoned her to death.

I'm not what you think.

The Americans offered freedom.

The Taliban offered money.

I fought without bullets,

made noises with my mouth,

spit up sand for my country,

became a thorn in the eyes

of an obscure enemy.

The Americans told me one thing,

the Qur'an something else.

Forgive me, friend,

if I don't shake your hand.

It's tied behind my back,

connected to the other side.

Huffing

He huffed salt up his nose
and watched his wife climb
out of the earth's ivory belly.

He is too high to swim,
frail against the open water.

Amy, do not jog
on the bridge at night.

She smiled and slammed
into the incoming headlights
of a blue Ford pickup.

He leaned over the rail
and dove into a prism
of one world refracting
the erratic image of another.

A Photo Journalist's Account
in Sudan

He paid a man 850 pounds to drive him to Darfur.

By evening the road turned bumpy.

Turn on the headlights.

No. Too dangerous.

Then stop the truck!

The journalist jumped out,

flipped on a flashlight.

Bodies covered the road.

A woman, slicked with grime,

carried away by flames and ash.

Quiet as monks,

they listened to silence.

The air spat bullets across the Bahr al-Arab River.

The driver dropped to the ground,

then taken—gone in a spray of blood and pain.

Metal liquefied his skin.

Sour heat rose from his chest.

He looked up at the sky with dead eyes.

Finally, the shooting stopped.

The journalist crawled to a tree,

prayed until he fell asleep.

OD

In the corner of my room

batteries stand like color guards

each with a metal spoon

waiting patiently for me to heat up

in the darkness

and pay homage to my fiery death.

Aphroditus Walks the Streets of Bimini

I hurry up the street to escape from shoeless,

half naked girls. A few bucks buys you a good time.

No one hears from you again if you're caught.

I slip inside a bar. Bob Marley singing

"Could You Be Loved" on the jukebox.

I breathe in the freedom of marijuana smoke

and watch two guys take bets on the ring toss.

A woman seated two chairs down sits next to me.

What are you drinking? she says.

Isn't that my line? I say.

She tips her head back and laughs.

Her icy teeth float in her black Russian mouth.

I point at her glass. The bartender

slides its twin into my hand.

I'm feeling dizzy after four drinks.

The woman and I go upstairs to a bedroom

decorated in red satin. There is a voodoo doll

sitting in a rocking chair with black lights

shooting fire out of its eyes.

The woman undresses.

Her body splits in half.

Her bare legs move about

like two mating garden snails.

I lick her toes.

Her mimetic muscles

stretch into a grin

and wrap my body

in gold-colored rum.

The pimp walks in and

covers my face with a pillow.

I sleep,

unafraid.

Killing Bin Laden

for the Quiet Professionals

Our weapons

spider legs patient.

Our eyes bloom jasmine.

We kill the man

that travels like wind.

Coworker's Birthday Party at Ziggie's Bar

Notes full of smoke clouds spit from the DJ.

Tom drinks at the opposite side of the bar.

He thinks he's John Wayne

and guns me down with his index finger.

He's an idiot. I flip him the bird

and jump into a glass of bourbon.

Tracy climbs a table orangutan-like.

She's an idiot, too.

I order another round.

And another. And another.

Tom guns me down again.

This time I give him a high five.

I call him Pilgrim.

I take Tracy's shirt off

and swing it around my head like a gladiator.

We end up in the back seat of my car,

blacked out like the lions of Rome.

Bataan Death March

We are a thin malarial line.

Fire trees shivering atheism.

In shit we march. Our faith

is a cheap tin can

kicked into a jungle mud hole.

A cloudy trail of river fog burns in the sun.

A water buffalo licks scum

from its nostrils, smacks flies with its tail.

The guards pick their teeth with a machete.

One of them flicks rice in my face. His breath

smells like warm chocolate cake.

I imagine my mom on the porch waving to me.

Alabama cotton grows from her fingers.

Methodist wood bathes in her bucketing voice.

All I can do is look up at the sky.

Confession

The monk is clicking a rosary

between his long suffering fingers

when I walk up and speak to him.

I confess life is a competition

and cut a woman off in Food Lion.

I feel a failure.

I confess I buy lots of stuff.

I feel deprived.

I confess my egotism

and hand a homeless man a dollar.

I feel insensible.

The monk points

to the tabernacle's undying flame.

In the pastoral light of his silent love

he teaches me much in so little time.

Siberian Hunter

It's cold in the Taiga.

Trees have their own language:

the first drop of rain.

The last star before the morning

reminds me to feed my dogs

and check the traps.

Thomas Merton Visits
Dollar General

I weep with Peter as the cock crows three times. I deny
my silence and go for a drive,
ending up at Dollar General. It opens in fifteen
minutes. Monks are early to everything.

I check my watch and then read my breviary to pass the
time. I am on my third Psalm
when the OPEN sign flashes red. It forces me to wonder
if a vacancy is waiting for me

in the life I left years ago, not the drinking and pot
smoking and reciting bad poetry in bars,
but the cosmic embrace of two teenagers running off to
kiss beneath the waves of honeysuckle.

At the heart of things, I love silence as much as I love
women, but by vow, I cannot have both.
I go inside the store to ponder this difficulty as if the
economy is the answer to everything.

Does happiness cost a dollar?

Monks are not saints. I flirt with the girl behind the
counter. I wonder what she'd look like
as a sunflower ransoming me from those walls of holy
madness, but wisdom drags me

back to the monastery before I can hold her hand. It teaches me to think of nothing. Only then

is monastic life bearable.

Paper Lanterns

The tsunami punched a hole

where my house once stood.

My refrigerator is jammed against a tree.

There is a dead girl inside.

I lean down and kiss her forehead

before the medic zips her body

in a plastic bag.

Pieces of metal are curled

like emergency blankets over the beach.

Bodies float ashore

like bobbing Geisha dolls.

Paper lanterns float above me

as my legs stitch a crooked seam across the beach.

The Bells of Balangiga

I

They killed everyone over ten.

Dimples of blood clung to the rice.

Smoke rolled up into the sky

and revealed a canal

overflowing with wet bones.

The Americans procured

the church bells as war trophies.

II

I arrived in Samar

a U.S. Peace Corps Volunteer 107 years later.

It was the first

I had heard of the massacre.

A priest ordered me to return the bells.

I listened patiently;

put it all in my report.

I never left the village.

I learned to speak Visayan

and drank gin until I no longer

remembered the past.

III

San Pedro Street, Los Angeles, CA

A homeless man

walks San Pedro Street

with his life packed inside a milk crate.

A young girl

sits on the curb

zipping and unzipping a jacket

and fiddles with hoody strings.

A street evangelist

passes out frayed Gideon Bibles.

A black man

sings a reggae song about Jesus.

Two volunteers

in front of the Midnight Mission

pass out white tube socks

and blue underwear.

The cop on the corner

checks his watch and wonders

who will steal a shopping cart.

An old woman with bony arms

herds a family of cats across the street.

No words come from her,

just the repairing breath of joy.

Xbox War Crimes

Flipping on the Xbox, I breathe electric air,

put on headphones and talk to my son

6,000 miles from Afghanistan.

I tell him about the real war,

the implacable effects it has on me.

I ask: *What do you know of hardship?*

He answers: *I miss my dad.*

I ask: *What do you know about war?*

He answers: *It's a game I like to play.*

I ask: *What do you know about death?*

He answers: *I dream of the day*

the plane comes to carry you home.

Three Drops of Wine

We must live each day, each minute of our life as though it is the last.

—Cardinal Nguyen Van Thuan

They arrested me for being a Christian.

Now I sit in Vinh Phu Prison and listen

to the Saigon River whisper

about the mission of suffering.

A few drops of wine on the palm of my hand

drip like sacred blood from Golgotha.

Prison is a test of faith,

the grotto of my enlightenment.

I close my eyes and see a crude beam strapped

to Christ's back against screams of doubt.

A coil of smoke rises from a candle.

White mushrooms grow on my bed.

Rice crawls out of my bowl.

On Assignment with *National Geographic*

I plop down in the dirt and shed my boots and socks

after walking half a day in Africa's Rift Valley.

A Maasi boy joins me. His shuka

is covered in earth and cow shit.

I offer him candy. He takes a bite. Smiles.

With his staff he peels back my tent flap

and looks inside to an excess of survival gear—

first aid kit; radio; emergency blanket—

and scratches his head.

Supai, I say. *Hi*.

He doesn't speak.

He digs out a handful of dates

from his deep pocket and tosses me one.

Ashe, I say. *Thank you.*

He sniffs my shoes.

His cheeks form

like talus cones at the base of his chin.

Then, just as he arrived, mysteriously,

he darts away, his naked feet

raking the bones of dynasties to the surface.

Chemo

A clump of hair

like a dead caterpillar

sticks to fingers.

Cough. Vomit. Headaches.

Weeks pass.

Sit in a leather chair.

Read the Bible.

Weeks pass.

Think about death.

Weeks pass.

Warm waters of the Jordan
pump through veins.

Little green pills fall from eyes.

Hair grows strong.

A field of olive trees.

Saint John's Hospital: Joplin, MO: Tornado, May 2011

The floor buckles

as if the Ozarks grow beneath it.

Patients rush the steps

like a brood of nervous chickens.

A crucifix hangs on a wall:

the finger of Jesus points the way out.

Rescue workers escort survivors

to tents that resemble a set of yellowed teeth.

Wheelchairs ear-ringed on trees.

The violent beauty of the sky glows tangerine.

Salem, Massachusetts, 1692

The minister's virgin daughter

studies a flock of black birds

hovering above an October moon.

A councilman spits cud in her eyes.

He claims she entertains the devil

and holds up his dead son as proof.

Puffy bodies sway

on nervous ropes after the trial.

Innocence hides in the weeds.

Plato's Retreat

for Larry Levenson

I spend weekends

on the waterbed

under the blue canopy

tied down by the rain

and the soft voice of Coney Island.

I caress the length of her arm.

My finger slips inside her.

Her lips moan, open and divine.

Tsalagi Arrowheads

Wandering through rows of tobacco,
leaves curled and yellowed by the sun,

I search for magical cuts of obsidian
as black as the eyes of the temple gods.

No trace at all. Only shadows stalking deer.
Stretching hides. Building river cane houses.

MS 13 Celebrating the Divine Savior of the World

Our hearts beat like a tombstone,

but we're not afraid to die

in this world we call home.

There are no strangers in heaven.

We are blessed.

The body of Jesus stands over us

with hands raised like weapons of mercy.

Fracking

If the Dakota prairie needs an icon,
then look no further than a tough
woman trucker hauling a million gallons
of salt water across Route 40
heading east above the subterranean rock
that pays her rent:

"All I can think about are my two little girls
a jobless thousand miles away in Newport.
I drive my eighteen-wheeler toward the horizon
of sexual fracking that rises above
the man camps like a virile cloud.
Men here believe they are Vikings.
I house a steel rod in my cab for those
who want to grab my waist
and pull me into their longhouse
thatched with nuru.
I open the hatch
to one of the salt water tanks.
I wish to be back in Rhode Island.
I can smell the ocean in my hair."

IV

Jonestown

I have tried my best to give you the life you've deserved,
but your disobedience has brought us here today.
If we cannot live in peace, then we will die in peace.
It is not suicide, but Christ the revolution,
a baptism not by fire, but by His blood crucified.

I am not blaming you, as Jesus did not blame Judas.
I tell you now, if you wish to go, go quickly,
and shake the corrupt hand of capitalism.
Congressman Ryan will wait for you,
but I cannot control my people.
They have gone out taking the guns with them.

I cannot protect you if you go.
Please, I forgive you, and I beg you stay,
if not for me, then for your wife and children.
Your boy has stopped crying. The medication is
working.
He is no longer afraid. And there, your wife, she sleeps.
Be a man and drink the wine.
Hold up your glass as Christ held up his arms for you.
Let's make a toast, for today you will be with me in
paradise.

Missing

The basement he kept us in
smelled like pee and dried leaves.

He said I was the prettier one,
touched me without permission.

What was I going to say?
No? Maybe later?

One morning I woke up
and he was next to me.

You're better than dope, he said,
then sniffed my breasts.

I pulled my sleepy arm away
from his sticky back, then got up
and watched the rain.

The other two girls watched me
with the blank stares of dolls.

They had never been
away from home without their parents.

Being a runaway has its advantages.

You learn to deal with creeps.

My father often touched me without permission.

The pregnant girl measured her belly,
determining how many days she had been missing.

The black-eyed girl rocked back and forth,
humming songs her mother used to sing to her as a
child.

Hearing her singing,
a cop stuck his head through the basement door,
saw us sitting by the furnace like three lumps of coal.

We got him, he said,
then reached out his hand.

I remember it having a calm grip.

Kurt Cobain Unplugged

He was controlled every second
by his past. Once, I asked him about it,
but Courtney told me I was hired
as a nanny, not a psychotherapist.

He was no bigger than a guitar pick,
a skinny geek that wrote songs in the woods.

He never loved Courtney.
Her thick voice, like dark beer
and cigarettes, frightened him.

In the end,
he decided to have an affair

with heroin and a shotgun.

After his death,
I touched Aberdeen's welcome sign:

Come As You Are.

Now I feel like he's part of me.

The Secrets of the Dead

No one was allowed to speak to the girl
giving birth on the side of the road.

No one was allowed
to pray over the stiff child's body.

The Pasha believed
the Armenians were lower than dogs.

Sold for forty pieces of silver,
my grandmother was lucky,

the resurrection of the sleeping rib,
the place where she stored her power.

Murder in Humboldt

for Brandon Teena

He called himself Brandon,
a tough name for a bag of bones.

He was a pretty little thing,
knew all the right words to say to a lady.

He was a great kisser,
but insisted on sleeping with his clothes on.

Someone found out *he* was a *she*
and showed her a good time in the back of a truck.

Sex is always consensual in a small town.

The sheriff didn't believe her rape story.

Days later a pair of bullets
found a home in the back of her head.

Her other life shivered out of its opaque skin
like an androgynous parrotfish,

her existence merging on the tip of a rainbow.

Leaving

A bruise ran down my shoulder
like ink spilling from a bottle.
He said he was sorry. Said it would
never happen again. But it happened again—
again and again and again.
Mom told me to leave.
I told her I could not
for the sake of the kids.
Crazy talk. Move in with me
if you have to, she said.
The following Sunday
Pastor Jim preached
that a little bit of David is in all of us.
We have our own giants to kill.
I dropped the kids off at Mom's house
and said I'd be back in a day or two.
I went home and made Joe a sandwich
and watched him eat it for a while
before hitting him across the head
with the skillet harder than the stone
that struck Goliath between the eyes,
the Valley of Elah now bloody on my kitchen floor.

The Hermit Kingdom

The concrete marker

that separates us from the rest of the world

is our great leader Kim Jong-un.

We collect salt for him as penance for our defected
husbands.

What lies on the other side of the 38th Parallel is
weakness.

You are no longer human the moment you cross it.

This is what we believe or we die in a mining accident.

We have no vocabulary to question our great leader.

He prohibits us from watching American TV

that speaks of freedom and Coca-Cola.

Dennis Rodman is our only American friend.

He is our friend because our great leader enjoys
basketball.

We will never be as tall as Dennis Rodman.

We will never be as fat as our great leader.

We do not complain about our empty bellies.

We praise our great leader for all he has done for us.

He gives us cows.

The cows give us shit.

The shit gives us leftover corn.

We eat the corn with a smile.

Pulling John Brzenk

I won my first title when I was eighteen.
Everyone lined up to shake my hand
like Caesar searching for the perfect soldier.
"I thought you'd be bigger," they said,
but I smiled, ignored their stares,
forearm pumped and ready for the world,
my fingers the strength of moon rock.

Locked in a hook, top roll, press,
my arms veined with the blood of my father,
flash strategies like two racing chariots.

I crush my opponents on the unforgiving table,
their biceps like torsion springs snapping.

I grew up above a bowling alley
and discovered my strength out of boredom.
Spent time bench pressing plastic echoes
on hard wood I believed would last forever.

Now every wrestler on the planet wants to pull me
and I imagine myself in a race flying over the top
of the latest demi-god wanting to be like me.

V

Growing Pains

I ran away from home
when I was three

an ancient nomad
hiding in the tobacco fields
from my drunk father

his calloused hands snapping
off a forsythia branch

then

smelling my heavy breath
he raises the branch high
above his head

striking my shadow again
and again and again.

The House No One Visited

Someone I know died of AIDS.

When I last saw Scotty thirty years ago

he was running after me with a baseball bat.

He threatened me every day after school.

He was much older than me, stronger.

He carried pain around him

like some boys carried .22 caliber rifles

to shoot innocent birds out of trees.

I shot my first rifle at thirteen.

My grandfather, a war vet, gave it to me.

My mother told me never to point it at anyone.

We should always greet our
neighbors with a smile, she said.

Not once did I smile at Scotty.

Grateful to Drill Sargent Harrison,

I no longer run from bullies.

Grateful to my mother,

I no longer hold a rifle in my hands.

I pray I never use what I know

as an instrument toward peace.

First Grade Stabbing in Art Class

When I was ten,

I stabbed Jeff McHenry with a pencil.

I didn't want him to know my name.

Secrets grew out of me like virulent blisters,

a gift sharpened years later overseas

working for the government.

Jeff clutched his arm.

The pain slowly discharged

from the cracks between his nosy fingers.

Bloodshot ammonia—
he often sniffed glass cleaner
from the janitor's closet—
crept from his soggy eyes.

When I returned home,

Mom said a little bird

revealed my sin.

A Shadow on a Mountain

The voice
of the Kentucky wilderness
cries out like a wild cat.

Drops of bourbon
stir the Barren River
where I drowned as a child.

So many years
before the spry breaths of her love
whispered to me the voice of God.

Chickamauga

Standing in the ditch
where the battlefield
digested my relative,

I listen in the quiet
to 4,000 unsettled boys
speaking their last words.

Reenactors breach a wall
of cedar trees and suddenly

everything is spattered
in smoke and conflict.

I peel back the fat
of a rotten stump,

dark as slavery,
expecting to find a bullet,

a button, a finger bone
of my dead relative,

or an answer
to why he fought.

As the sun goes down
over the battlefield,

his voice rises
from the ground,

like moist heat accepting
the bone-dry shouts

of a lost cause.

Hiking in Winter Woods Behind My House

A tree falls
over a large gulley.

The water rafts
beneath a thick layer
of snow and ice.

The tree cracks
like dead bone.

My head
goes off like a gun,

sends splinters
of frozen wreckage
into the piercing air.

Hoarfrost grows
viciously on my coat.

My pupils:
two black moor fish
swimming wildly.

My blood freezes
thick in the glacial water.

Enough panic.

Return home.

Run to the fire.

Playing Dodgeball on a Trampoline

Steel limbs and flaked springs.

No cushions. Tougher boys

back then, our lanky bodies

like tangled wisteria clashing.

The apple-colored ball

rocketed past my head.

Jason crushed my arm

against the wet grass,

my elbow opposing the joint,

my eyes damp with curiosity.

I ran home, held up my arm,

showed Mother the trophy I had earned.

Hunting Deer with Green Berets

We hiked a dirt trail

the Cherokees once used

as an escape route to the mountains.

I wondered if Andrew Jackson knelt

on this inviolable parcel before God

and asked forgiveness for the death march he decreed.

No one spoke, as if in remembrance of what occurred
here.

Silently, we took positons overlooking a cornfield.

We waited patiently in the tedious dark

until the sun caught our cold breath.

We watched it flatten out in the sky.

After a while, a snooping doe, grunting,

eased her way toward the smell of corn.

Her coarse tongue slid across dry nostrils.

Fragrant leaves hitched to her warm body.

I honored her ancestral blood

with an arrow through the chest.

I removed her pulsating heart

held it above my head

like a quiet professional.

We dragged the fatty corpse

away into the rising light.

Behold the Man

1.

Out of obedience

I accepted a berretta
in one hand
and a Bible in the other.

In the house where I lived,
saints and war medals
were displayed on walls.

Years later,
eating chow in a dirt hut,
I decide to enter a monastery.

2.

On the lawn
outside my window,
I watch a fidgety robin
search for worms
as I envision the life
I must lead in this invisible world.

3.

Inside the church,
the wind whispers
the stillness of dawn,
chants words
in the language of Popes.

4.

My fourth year
conceived in secret,
I leave the monastery
and relocate to the American Rome
where everyone listens
under water,
where the world shouts
and cannot be heard.

My Favorite Color Is Black

We stand inside the darkness
like a tombstone or monument.

I unlock her chignon hair.
It gathers on the nape
of her neck like crows nesting.

Because the brotherhood
sees me kiss her, they say:
make your bones.

Because her father
speaks bleakly, she says:
hang me from a tree.

Up till now
people feared it
but death admits defeat
and we gather rain
in the cotton fields for days
until my skin turns black
and the past no longer sleeps.

For My Ex-Wife

I returned home
and she was gone.

Nothing but a note
on the coffee table:

Take care.

My arrested emotions
like an impatient winter storm.

It was good she left.
I no longer grind
my teeth at night.

I no longer look
into her visa-green eyes.

My note to her:

Set fire to my heart.
Watch it burn.
But know my blood is strong
and vinegar to taste.

How quickly people divorce;
how one moment you're walking
hand in hand, the next
sleeping on a stack
of smoldering stones.

Thin Red Line—D.C. Metro

I crossed the line often

with little resistance.

Once or twice

junkies asked for money.

Suspicion kept me brave.

But tonight,

halfway down the platform,

I notice a man

curled deceptively quiescent

against the vaulted ceiling.

Inside his hoody:

an obscure face serpentine.

The platform clock ticks two minutes.

The oily heat

from the approaching train

blisters my nostrils.

The man walks toward me.

His frosty breath is visible.

Silent words open his chapped lips.

I reach for my baton

secretly tucked inside my jacket.

The train arrives with a wind surge.

Doors open.

I'm absorbed in a smelly mixture

of body odor and Chinese takeout.

The train coughs and pitches forward.

The man walks tight-fistedly away.

I watch him until my muscles relax.

My empty hand crawls out of my jacket.

Walking Along the James River

I talk to the water

because I am shy to God.

White water cuddles

avocado-colored rocks

beached at the shore's lip.

Barefoot, I climb to the top

of the highest rock

and listen to the river speak

in acute whispers about my past

that only Daemons know.

It moves about

like a damp snake tongue

hunting a fatuous rodent,

swallowing it whole

as time digests my secrets

less than a step to immortality.

A Knock at the Door

The sun cried in 1915.

It cries today.

Armenia.

My host mother Valia

and I are having coffee

looking at old photos,

one of which revisits me

every day since my service

of her grandmother

before the Turks knocked

on the door and stuffed mohair

in her bleeding mouth

and marched her

across the prejudiced desert.

They say she was unrecognizable

when she arrived in Deir-el-Zor,

now an extinct Syrian camp

where a mass grave of bones

clatter in the dust

to awaken the grief observed

in Valia's sturdy blue eyes

and the forgiveness expressed

in the gentle grip of her hand.

We sit there

silently mourning

the good that was lost.

Orphans of the Pacific

When I landed in Manila,

orphaned raindrops fell from the sky.

Morning brought bay smells

of clammy children and yesterday's garbage.

An old man was sitting on a bench.

I touched his hand to my forehead

and asked for a blessing. His smile

faded to black and I turned

just in time to see a young boy

disappear beneath a cluster

of pink plastic bags.

He's looking for his parents,

the old man said.

He pointed to a shack,

its eastern wall now drifting

toward a synthetic island of Coke bottles.

Storm blew them out to sea.

The boy, now smiling,

surfaced, holding a slipper in his hand.

We watched him dive a second time

in search of one more piece of hope.

Metro Manila—Red Light District

A shifty alley of barbeque joints.

An old lady stretches out her vine-like arm.

Her mauve hands hold two strip-show tickets.

You have good time, she said.

Her lips point toward a balcony

where girls in cozy dresses

perch themselves on ledges

like clipped winged parrots,

beautiful bodies all of them,

high above my uplifted hands

that held two tickets

burning like populist effigies.

Bullied in a Chinese Shoe Shop

When our bodies met,

you stood there

like a stiff island

with eyes burned dark

by the mulish sun,

clumsily pulled your gun.

I shrugged,

narrowed my eyes, and said:

You live because the child

in your craven arms woke up

and requested a blessing

from my foreign hand.

Tombstone Inscription

My last words to the world

discharged silence,

like humility hemorrhaging.

In heaven, there is a book of names

as holy as they are invisible.

Acknowledgments

Grateful acknowledgment is made to the editors of the following publications in which versions of many of the poems from this collection first appeared:

Emerge Literary Journal, *CityLitRag*, *Atticus Review*, *A-Minor Magazine*, *Muddy River Poetry Review*, *Gravel*, *Dappled Things*, *Noctua Review*, *Bitterzoet Magazine*, *Long Story Short*, *Scapegoat Review*, *Wilderness House Literary Review*, *Emerge Literary Journal*, *Coe Review*, *The Transnational*, and *Buddhist Poetry Review*

"Coworker's Birthday Party at Ziggie's Bar" appeared originally as "Surly" in *Boston Literary Review*.

"Paper Lanterns" appeared originally as "The Origin of the Sun" in *Cha: An Asian Literary Journal*, issue 18.

"Operation Iraqi Freedom, 2003" appeared originally as "Iraq" in *Off the Coast*.

"Benazir Bhutto" was shortlisted in the poetry contest, Betrayal, sponsored by *Cha: An Asian Literary Journal*, and appeared in the June 2013 issue.

"The Secrets of the Dead" appeared in *The Land of the Four Rivers: My Experience as a US Peace Corps Volunteer in Armenia (2006-2008)*. The poetry collection was published by Cervena Barva Press in 2012. Several poems in the collection were nominated for a 2013 Pushcart Prize. Additionally, the collection won the 2013 Best Poetry Book from Peace Corps Writers.

I would like to thank Baron Wormser and Loren Kleinman for their invaluable critique and editorial skill. Without their guidance, these poems would not have been possible.

About the Author

Matthew A. Hamilton is a former soldier, Congressional aide, U.S. Peace Corps volunteer, and Benedictine monk. He is a three-time Pushcart Prize nominee and his stories and poems have appeared in a variety of national and international journals, such as *Boston Literary Magazine* and *Atticus Review*. Matthew is currently the librarian for Benedictine College Preparatory in Richmond, VA.